The Meaning Behind the Magic

The Symbols of Christmas

Written by Diane Kann

Illustrated by

Mary Grace Victoria

Kannceptual Creations

Paws to Read – A moment shared is a memory made.

Visit us at: *boltandcharliebooks.com*

Published by Kannceptual Creations LLC

An imprint of Bolt and Charlie Books

boltandcharliebooks.com

Illustrations by Mary Grace Victoria

ISBN: 978-1-969569-42-5

Printed in the United States of America

First Edition, November 2025

Paws to Read is a Bolt and Charlie Books initiative promoting early literacy and shared storytime experiences.

Table of Contents

PART I - Faith and Wonder

The Star of Bethlehem   2

The Manger   4

The Angels   6

The Shepherd's Staff   8

The Three Gifts   10

The Candle   12

PART II - Nature and Renewal

The Evergreen Tree   16

The Wreath   18

Holly and Ivy   20

The Poinsettia   22

The Snowflake   24

The Yule Log   26

PART III Joy and Celebration

The Bells   30

Caroling and Song   32

Christmas Cards and Letters   34

Gift Giving and Wrapping   36

The Feast and Table   38

Lights and Lanterns   40

PART IV Traditions and Togetherness

Stockings   44

The Tree Topper   46

Gingerbread and Cookies   48

The Christmas Morning Gift   50

The Dove   52

The Advent Calendar   54

Traditions Around the World   57

Our Family Traditions   69

The Light We Share   76

PART I
Faith and Wonder

"When the path feels uncertain, look to the light. Follow where faith and wonder lead."

The Star of Bethlehem – A Light to Lead the Way

The Star of Bethlehem

A Light to Lead the Way

Long ago, a single star pierced the darkness above Bethlehem, shining brighter than all others. Wise travelers watched the sky and followed its steady glow until it rested above a humble stable.

The Star of Bethlehem reminds us that even in uncertain times, a light of hope can guide us home.
Many families place a star at the top of their tree — a symbol of faith and guidance. It speaks of direction, but also of wonder: how a small point of light can change the world.

When we see stars twinkling on quiet December nights, we remember that every journey has a guiding light — if we lift our eyes to see it.

"In the simplest places, love finds its way. That's where peace is born."

The Manger – Love in a Humble Place

The Manger

Love in a Humble Place

It wasn't a palace or a grand hall that welcomed the first Christmas. It was a manger — a feeding trough for animals, lined with hay.

There, among gentle creatures and quiet breath, the Christ Child was laid. The manger teaches that love often enters the world quietly, in places we least expect.

Families who set up nativity scenes remember this: that greatness is not measured by gold or power, but by kindness and compassion.

Each small figure — shepherd, angel, and child — becomes a story of peace made simple. The manger whispers: love begins wherever there is room.

"When hearts open, joy takes flight.
We become the messengers of light."

The Angels – Messengers of Joy

The Angels

Messengers of Joy

O n that first Christmas night, shepherds in the fields looked up to see a sky filled with light. Angels appeared, singing, "Peace on earth, goodwill toward all."

The word *angel* means "messenger," and their message has never faded. Angels remind us that joy is meant to be shared — not kept hidden.

Many families hang angel ornaments or place one atop the tree to remember that we, too, can be bearers of good news: through kind words, gentle actions, and helping hands.

When we listen closely to music or laughter during the season, we can almost hear the echo of those ancient songs — joy still ringing through the night.

"To guide with kindness is the greatest gift.
Every gentle act lights the way."

The Shepherd's Staff – Kindness and Care

The Shepherd's Staff

Kindness and Care

The shepherd's staff, curved at the top, guided and protected the flock. In Christmas traditions, it became the model for the candy cane — sweet and striped like the shepherd's crook.

The red symbolizes love and sacrifice; the white, purity and peace.

Every time we hang a candy cane on the tree or share one with a friend, it's more than a treat — it's a symbol of caring for others.

The shepherd's staff reminds us to look after those around us, to lift someone who's fallen behind, and to lead with gentleness. In doing so, we become shepherds of kindness in our own small world.

"True giving isn't measured by worth.
It's the love behind the gift that lasts."

The Three Gifts
Gold, Frankincense, and Myrrh

The Three Gifts

Gold, Frankincense, and Myrrh

The wise men brought treasures fit for a king: gold for value, frankincense for prayer, myrrh for healing. Yet the child who received them lay in straw.

Their gifts remind us that true worth is not in what we give, but in the love behind it.

Today, as we wrap presents and tie ribbons, we echo their journey of generosity. Each gift — big or small — can carry meaning if it is offered with care.

The Magi's gifts still speak: give wisely, love deeply, and remember that every act of giving can become a holy thing.

"One flame can chase the dark away.
Hope begins with a single light."

The Candle — Light in the Darkness

The Candle

Light in the Darkness

L ong before electric bulbs twinkled in windows, candles were lit to celebrate hope.

In churches and homes, a single flame might stand for peace, another for joy, another for love. Together, they became the Advent candles — small lights growing brighter as Christmas draws near.

A candle's glow reminds us that darkness is never final. One light can spark another, and soon the whole room shines.

When we light candles or switch on tiny lights along our mantels, we take part in that same tradition — choosing light over shadow, warmth over fear, and hope over despair.

PART II
Nature and Renewal

(Life Everlasting and the Quiet Wisdom of Creation)

The Evergreen Tree – Life That Endures

"Seasons change, but life holds on.
Hope is the color that never fades."

The EvergreenTree

Life That Endures

When the world turns cold and bare, the evergreen tree stays bright and green. Long before Christmas, people brought evergreens indoors to remind themselves that life continues through every season.

Christians later saw it as a symbol of eternal life — hope that never fades.

Each time we decorate a tree, we echo that ancient joy. Every twinkling light and ornament becomes a reminder that even in winter's stillness, something living endures.

The evergreen whispers, *Life finds a way to bloom again.*

"One circle, endless grace.
Where love begins, it never ends."

The Wreath – Love Without End

Holly and Ivy

Strength Through Every Season

Holly, with its sharp leaves and bright berries, and ivy, with its gentle climbing green, have decorated homes for centuries. In cold months, they remain alive, symbols of endurance and faith.

The red berries recall the joy and sacrifice of love; the green leaves, the promise of renewal.

Holly protects; ivy clings and connects — two sides of the same gift. Together, they tell us that beauty and strength often grow side by side.

When we weave holly and ivy into garlands, we carry a little piece of the forest's courage into our homes.

*"A single act of love can shine.
Even the smallest gift becomes a miracle."*

The Poinsettia – The Gift of Kindness

The Poinsettia

The Gift of Kindness

In Mexico, long ago, a girl wanted to bring a gift to her church on Christmas Eve but had no money for flowers. She gathered green weeds from the roadside, and as she placed them before the altar, they bloomed into brilliant red stars.

Those flowers became the poinsettia, now known around the world as the *Flor de Nochebuena* — the Flower of the Holy Night.

Its red leaves remind us that small acts of love can become something beautiful.
When we share kindness, we too make miracles bloom

"Each pattern tells a story of its own.
Even in winter, every heart can shine."

The Snowflake – Every One Unique

The Yule Log

Warmth in the Long Night

Before Christmas trees, people celebrated with the burning of the Yule log — a great piece of wood placed in the hearth to welcome warmth and drive away darkness.

Families gathered around the fire, telling stories, singing songs, and sharing food. A small piece of the log was saved to light next year's flame, linking one celebration to the next.

The Yule log reminds us that every flame we kindle connects us to those who came before — and to those who will come after.

Its crackle and glow whisper: *Light returns. Warmth remains.*

PART III
Joy and Celebration

(Sounds and Sharing that
Fill the Season with Light)

The Bells – Rings of Joy

*"Every chime carries light and laughter.
Joy is meant to echo through the world."*

The Bells

Rings of Joy

From steeples, sleighs, and little hands shaking shiny silver bells, the sound of ringing fills the air each Christmas.

Bells have long called people to gather — to worship, to celebrate, to rejoice. Their bright tones break through the hush of winter and remind us that joy was meant to be shared.

In old traditions, bells also chased away darkness, their music protecting homes from sorrow.

When we hear bells ringing on Christmas Eve, they seem to carry laughter, memory, and hope through the cold night — each chime a promise that light has returned once again.

Caroling and Song – Voices Together

"Every chime carries light and laughter.
Joy is meant to echo through the world."

Caroling and Song

Voices Together

O nce, people carried lanterns door to door, singing carols to share warmth and cheer. The songs told stories of angels, shepherds, and love that never ends.

Music unites us — whether it's a family around a piano, a choir in church, or a single voice humming softly while wrapping gifts.

Each song is a thread connecting past and present, weaving hearts together through melody.
When we sing, we give shape to joy itself — and sometimes, even the stars seem to listen.

Merry Christmas!

Happy Holidays!

Christmas Cards and Letters – Love in an Envelope

*"A few words can travel far.
Love, once written, never fades."*

Christmas Cards and Letters

Love in an Envelope

A handwritten note, a folded card, a child's careful drawing — these small messages travel farther than we imagine.

Christmas cards began centuries ago as a way to send blessings to distant friends. Today, they still carry the same simple truth: someone remembered you.

Whether sent by mail or made by hand, each card is a spark of connection in a busy world.

When we open one, we open a moment of love — proof that kindness can fit inside an envelope.

Gift Giving and Wrapping – The Joy of Sharing

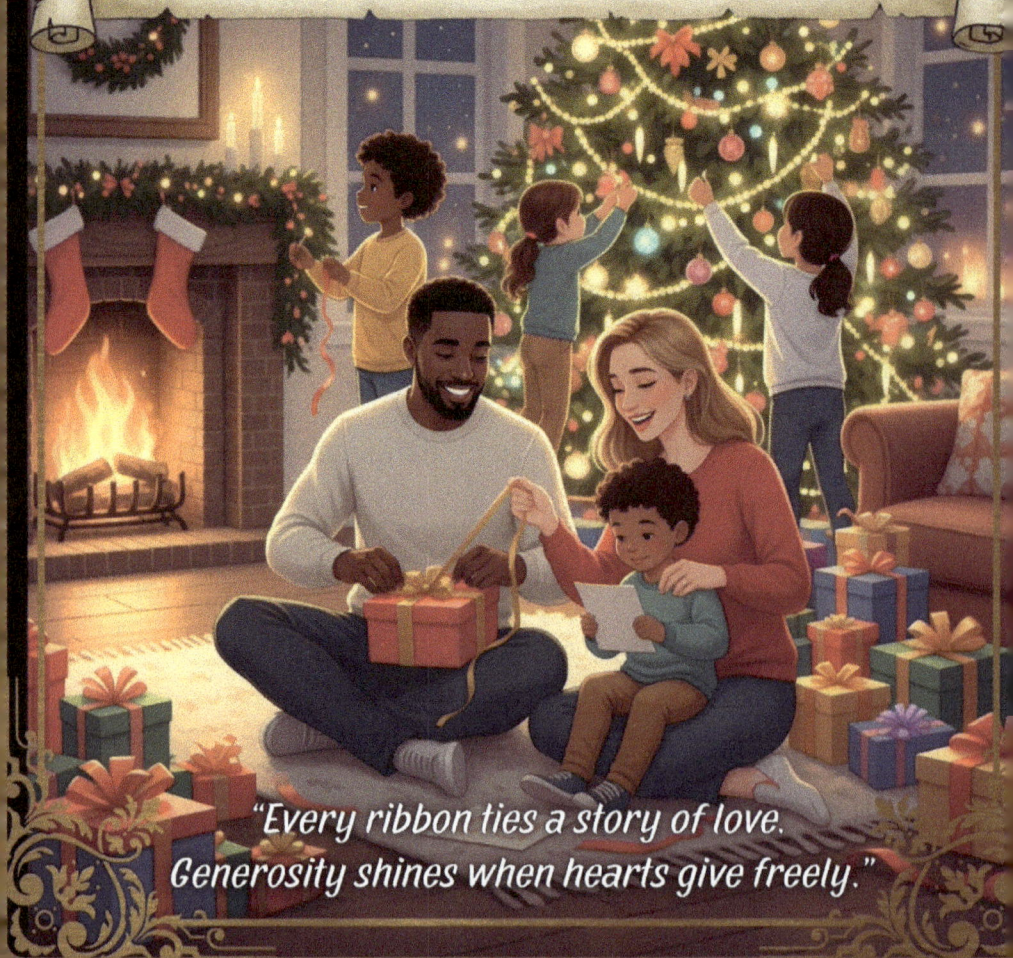

"Every ribbon ties a story of love.
Generosity shines when hearts give freely."

Gift Giving and Wrapping

The Joy of Sharing

T he first Christmas gifts were carried across deserts by wise men following a star.

Now, we wrap ours in paper and ribbon — the excitement of surprise hiding within.

But the real magic isn't in what's inside the box; it's in the thought that someone chose it just for us.

Giving becomes an act of love, a way to say "You matter to me."

As we tie each bow and slip gifts beneath the tree, we remember: generosity shines brightest when given freely.

The Feast and Table – Gathering in Gratitude

*"A table becomes sacred when we pray.
Gratitude turns every meal into cherished moments."*

The Feast and Table

Gathering in Gratitude

All around the world, families celebrate with food — from roast dinners to sweet breads and warm drinks.

At every table, laughter and stories mix with the scent of spices and the glow of candles.

The Christmas meal is more than a feast; it's a symbol of community, of hearts made full by gratitude.

Every chair, even the empty ones, holds a memory.

When we give thanks before eating, we honor those who came before and those yet to come — a circle of blessing shared in every meal.

Lights and Lanterns – Shining in the Dark

"Each glow tells the story of hope.
It shines, and the world grows bright."

Lights and Lanterns

Shining in the Dark

L ong before electric bulbs, people lit candles in windows to guide travelers home.

Today, strings of lights sparkle on trees, rooftops, and porches — little galaxies born of joy.

Lights remind us that darkness cannot win when love is near.

Each tiny glow, from a lantern to a glittering street, tells the same story: hope spreads, one light at a time.

When we plug in the first strand or light a candle at dusk, we take part in an ancient promise — that the world will never be without light again.

Stockings

Gifts of Secret Kindness

The story tells of Saint Nicholas, who slipped coins into stockings left to dry beside a hearth, helping a family in need without ever being seen.

From that legend grew our own tradition of hanging stockings and filling them with small surprises.

Each stocking is a promise that generosity doesn't need applause — only a willing heart.

When we tuck gifts inside while the world sleeps, we keep the spirit of Saint Nicholas alive: quiet giving, joy in secret, love without announcement.

The Tree Topper – Star or Angel Above All

"Guided by light, lifted by grace.
Hope shines highest when love leads the way."

The Tree Topper

Star or Angel Above All

A t the very top of the Christmas tree, one symbol rises highest — a star that recalls Bethlehem's light or an angel that carried glad tidings.

Whichever we choose, it crowns the tree with meaning: guidance and grace.

The star reminds us to follow hope wherever it leads; the angel, to listen for messages of peace.

When the topper is placed last, a hush often fills the room.

It's a moment of completion — our decorations become a prayer that every home may be watched over by light.

Gingerbread and Cookies
Sweet Stories of Love

"Each crumb tells a memory, each scent a song.
Where love is shared, joy lingers long."

The Christmas Morning Gift

Wonder Awakens

B efore the wrapping is torn and ribbons scatter, there is a heartbeat of stillness — the pause before discovery.

That moment is the real gift: the look of awe, the gasp of delight, the laughter that follows.

Giving and receiving become the same joy mirrored in two hearts.

Whether it's something handmade or something hoped for, the first gift of Christmas morning is always wonder itself — the reminder that love still surprises us.

Peace on Earth

"Peace begins on quiet wings.
It grows when kindness calms the world."

The Dove – Peace Made Visible

The Dove

Peace Made Visible

White and gentle, the dove has been a symbol of peace for centuries.

When it appears among holiday decorations, it carries the message first sung by angels: "Peace on Earth."

To hang a dove ornament or draw one in snow is to declare our hope for a world where every voice is heard and every home is safe.

Peace begins small — in forgiveness, in a soft word, in hands that choose to build instead of break.

The dove teaches that true strength flies on quiet wings.

The Advent Calendar – Waiting with Joy

"Peace begins on quiet wings.
It grows when kindness calms the world."

The Advent Calendar

Waiting with Joy

December is a month of waiting — candles counted, doors opened, tiny surprises revealed.

The Advent calendar turns waiting into wonder, teaching patience as each day brings a spark of joy. Behind every window is a reminder that good things grow slowly — hope, kindness, and love most of all.

When we reach the final day and open the last door, we see the greatest gift of Christmas: the journey itself, step by step, made bright by expectation.

Traditions Around the World

(How Christmas Shines in Many Lands)

Germany

Candles, Wreaths, and Markets of Light

GERMANY

Candles, Wreaths,
and Markets of Light

In Germany, families gather each week of Advent to light candles on a green wreath — one flame for each Sunday before Christmas. In towns and villages, wooden stalls glow with lanterns and the scent of cinnamon. These *Christkindl* markets are places of warmth in the cold, where friends share music, laughter, and gingerbread hearts.

The Advent wreath reminds everyone that light grows brighter when shared.

Mexico

Las Posadas and The Poinsettia's Gift

ITALY

La Befana and the Joy of Giving

In Italy, an old legend tells of La Befana, a kind woman who missed her chance to visit the Christ Child. Each year she flies on her broom, leaving small gifts for sleeping children so she will never miss another. Families also share a great Christmas Eve meal called *La Vigilia*, celebrating togetherness and hope. From Italy we learn that it's never too late to give love away.

Philippines

The Lanterns of Light

PHILIPPINES

The Lanterns of Light

In the Philippines, giant star-shaped lanterns called *parols* brighten the December nights. They symbolize the Star of Bethlehem guiding the way. Churches hold early-morning masses called *Simbang Gabi*, where families gather in prayer and song before dawn. When the lanterns glow, they carry one message: faith shines brightest when people come together.

Sweden

St. Lucia Day and the Crown of Candles

Our Family Traditions

(Pages for Your family to Write or Draw Your Own Stories)

Page 1

What Makes Our Christmas Special

Every family celebrates in its own way. Some gather by the fire, some sing, some help neighbors or rescue animals, some bake favorite treats. Write or draw what makes your family's Christmas special.

- What traditions do we repeat every year?

- Who starts decorating first?

- What song or story means the most to us?

Page 2

Our Symbols of Christmas

T he symbols in this book are part of everyone's story —
but some have special meaning for you.

Our favorite ornament:

A decoration that reminds us of someone we love

Our favorite Christmas food or scent:

*You can draw, paste photos, or write memories here — so they
shine again each year.*

Page 3

Looking Forward

C hristmas is not only remembering the past; it's creating what comes next.

1. What new tradition would we like to begin?

2. What kind act could become part of our yearly celebration?

3. How can we share light with others in the year ahead?

The Light We Share

The Light We Share

The first Christmas began with light — a star, a candle, a newborn hope.

That light has never gone out. It flickers in every kindness, glows in every gathering, and shines in every heart that chooses peace.

When we decorate, sing, give, and remember, we carry that same flame forward.

May your home be filled with warmth, your days with wonder, and your nights with quiet joy.

And may the light you share this Christmas guide someone else along their way.

www.ingramcontent.com/pod-product-compliance
Lightning Source LLC
Chambersburg PA
CBHW062024040426
42447CB00010B/2130